Clara SCHUMANN

by Joanne Mattern
with Consultation by John Viscardi,
Executive Director of Classic Lyric Arts
illustrated by Marilena Perilli

Egremont, Massachusetts

Classical Composers has been produced and published by Red Chair Press Books for Young Readers:
Red Chair Press LLC   PO Box 333   South Egremont, MA 01258
www.redchairpress.com

 Download a Free Activity Guide on our website.

For more information about Classic Lyric Arts, visit www.classiclyricarts.org.

Names: Mattern, Joanne, 1963- author. | Viscardi, John, consultant. | Perilli, Marilena, illustrator.

Title: Clara Schumann / by Joanne Mattern, with consultation by John Viscardi, executive director of Classic Lyric Arts ; illustrated by Marilena Perilli.

Description: Egremont, Massachusetts : Red Chair Press, [2025] | Series: Classical composers | Interest age level: 007-010. | Includes bibliographical references and index. | Summary: Clara Schumann (1819–1896), a German pianist and composer, was a prominent figure in the Romantic era ... Colorful illustrations plus photographs of meaningful sites and settings connect readers to important points in Schumann's history. A timeline and B Sharp sidebars add details to the composer's life story.--Publisher.

Identifiers: ISBN: 978-1-64371-436-3 (LB hardcover) | 978-1-64371-437-0 (paperback) | 978-1-64371-439-4 (S&L ebook) | LCCN: 2024936082

Subjects: LCSH: Schumann, Clara, 1819-1896--Juvenile literature. | Women composers--Germany--Biography--Juvenile literature. | CYAC: Schumann, Clara, 1819-1896. | Composers-- Germany--Biography. | LCGFT: Biographies. | BISAC: JUVENILE NONFICTION / Biography & Autobiography / Music. | JUVENILE NONFICTION / Biography & Autobiography / Performing Arts. | JUVENILE NONFICTION / Music / Classical. | JUVENILE NONFICTION / Biography & Autobiography / Women.

Classification: LCC: ML417.S4 M38 2025 | DDC: 780.92--dc23

Copyright © 2026 Red Chair Press LLC
RED CHAIR PRESS, the RED CHAIR and associated logos are
registered trademarks of Red Chair Press LLC.

All rights reserved. No part of this book may be reproduced, stored in an information or retrieval system, or transmitted in any form by any means, electronic, mechanical including photocopying, recording, or otherwise without the prior written permission from the Publisher. For permissions, contact info@redchairpress.com

Image credits: Cover, pp. 4, 11, 12, 20, 26 © Shutterstock; pp. 4, 6, 24 © Lebrecht Music Arts/Bridgeman Images; pp. 12, 27 © A. Dagli Orti/© NPL - DeA Picture Library/Bridgeman Images; p. 20 © Bridgeman Images; p. 31 © Martin Allen. All rights reserved 2023/Bridgeman Images

Illustrations: Marilena Perilli, except p. 7 by Joe LeMonnier

Printed in the United States of America

0425 1P CGF25

Table of Contents

A Child at the Piano 4

A Young Performer 12

Love and Marriage 20

Clara on Her Own 26

Timeline 30

Glossary 32

Read More 32

Index 32

A Child at the Piano

During the 1800s, almost all the famous **composers** were men. It was very unusual for a woman to be a highly thought of composer or musician. Clara Schumann was different. She started as a child **prodigy**. Later she became a famous composer.

Clara Wieck was born on September 13, 1819. She was born in Leipzig, Saxony in today's Germany. Clara's mother, Mariane, was a talented singer and piano teacher. Her father, Friedrich, was a piano teacher too. The Wieck house was full of music.

B# **B SHARP:** Clara's mother often sang at a famous concert hall in Leipzig called the Gewandhaus.

When Clara was five years old, her parents divorced. Clara's mother moved away. Clara stayed in Leipzig with her father. She and her mother wrote letters to each other, but they did not see each other very often.

Clara loved to play the piano. Her father knew she had a lot of talent. He believed she could be a famous piano player.

Clara's father gave her music lessons. He was very strict. Every day, they spent an hour doing lessons. Clara learned piano, violin, and singing. She even learned how to write music. Then, after a few years, Clara had to practice two hours every day.

Clara did not go to school with other children. Her father taught her some of the most important subjects. But mostly she spent each day learning music.

A Young Performer

When Clara Wieck was nine years old, she had her first public **performance**. She played piano at the Gewandhaus. There were many other performers at that concert, so Clara only played for a short time.

Later that year, Clara played a concert at the house of a family friend. There she met a young man named Robert Schumann. Robert was also a piano student. He had come to Leipzig to study piano with Clara's father. Clara and Robert became good friends.

In 1830, Clara performed her first solo concert at the Gewandhaus. She was 11 years old. Clara played many different pieces. Most were written by other composers. But she did have the chance to play a few pieces she had composed herself.

Audiences were amazed by the compositions Clara wrote as well as by her playing. News of her talents spread among the music-lovers of Germany and other parts of Europe.

B# **B SHARP:** Clara liked to perform **improvisations**. Improvisations were very popular at concerts at the time. Performers would change introductions to pieces, take flexible approaches to tempo and rhythm, and even create their own versions of other composers' works. Clara did all these things. In many ways, Clara helped create the style of "Classical Music" we know today.

Clara's father was pleased at how well she was performing. In 1832, he decided to take Clara on a tour of Paris. Clara performed in many places. Her father controlled everything about her performance. He even made her wear all-white dresses so she would be easily seen and remembered on stage.

Clara's father hoped Clara would become famous in Paris. However, his plans did not work out. After just a few months, Clara and her father returned home to Leipzig.

B SHARP: Clara began writing her most famous piece when she was only 13. It was called "Piano **Concerto** in A minor."

In 1837, Clara went to Vienna, Austria. People in Vienna loved music. Clara played many concerts there. Famous composers and writers of the time came to hear her play. Frédéric Chopin and Franz Liszt encouraged people to go hear her play.

Clara stayed in Vienna for about five months. One music critic said, "In her creative hands, the most ordinary passage… acquires a significant meaning, a color."

B# **B SHARP:** Clara was one of the first important performers to play music from **memory** instead of using sheet music.

Love and Marriage

While Clara was performing in Vienna, Robert Schumann was still studying music with Clara's father. He even lived with the family for a time. Soon, Clara and Robert fell in love. In 1837, Robert asked Clara to marry him. She said yes. But her father said no.

Robert and Clara took her father to court. The judge agreed that the couple could get married. However, they waited until Clara was 21 years old. At that age, she did not need her father's permission. In 1840, Robert and Clara got married.

Clara and Robert wrote music together. They also kept a **journal**. They wrote about their lives and feelings. In the journal they wrote personal notes to each other.

Robert and Clara both loved a poem called "If You Love for Beauty." For Robert's 31st birthday, Clara wrote music to the poem and gave it to him as a present. She also wrote music for him as a Christmas present.

Robert Schumann is known as a great composer, too. Most of his famous works were written about 1839–1840. Clara, however was seen to be the more talented musician.

Shown here are six of the Schumanns' eight children, about 1853.

Clara and Robert had eight children together. Clara did not let being a wife and mother stop her from performing. She and Robert toured Europe together. She also performed solo concerts.

Then, in 1844, Robert got sick. His mental health became very bad. Robert could not sleep. He cried all the time. Clara stopped performing to take care of her husband.

 B SHARP: Clara continued to write music when she had the chance while taking care of her family.

Clara on Her Own

In 1853, a young musician came to visit the Schumanns. His name was Johannes Brahms. When Brahms began playing for Robert, he rushed to get Clara so she could hear Brahms, too. The three of them became great friends. Robert and Clara taught Brahms a lot about writing music. He would later become a famous composer as well.

Clara and Robert had some happy times. But Robert was still very sick. In 1854, he went to stay at a mental hospital. Only two years later, in 1856, Robert died.

Clara composed a variety of music: full symphonies for an orchestra, chamber music, and pieces for one piano.

Clara only composed one piece of music after Robert died. But she kept on performing. She often did concerts with a famous violinist named Joseph Joachim. Clara toured all over Europe. She performed with many other musicians and also taught younger students wherever her tour took her.

In 1896, Clara Schumann died in Frankfurt, Germany at age 77. For a while, her music was forgotten. Later however, she became popular again. Her music is enjoyed by people all over the world.

B SHARP: Clara and Brahms remained good friends. He often took care of her children while she went on tour.

Important Dates in Clara Schumann's Life

1819   Clara Wieck is born in Leipzig, Germany.

1825   Clara's parents divorce; her father begins giving her music lessons.

1828   Young Clara gives her first public performance; she meets Robert Schumann.

1832   Clara and her father travel to Paris.

1837   Clara travels to Vienna, where she becomes very popular.

1840   Clara and Robert Schumann marry.

1854   Robert Schumann, Clara's husband, enters a mental hospital.

1856   Robert Schumann dies at age 46.

1896   Clara Schumann dies on May 20.

This monument marks the grave site for Robert and Clara Schumann in Bonn, Germany.

Glossary

composers people who write music

concerto a musical piece for an orchestra

improvisations music composed on the spot, without being written beforehand

journal a daily record of news and events; a diary

memory remembering information

performance a public show or concert

prodigy someone who is very talented; a genius

Read More About Schumann

Reich, Susanna. *Clara Schumann: Piano Virtuoso.* Clarion Books, 1999.

Index

Brahms, Johannes 26, 29
Chopin, Frédéric 19
Germany, Frankfurt 29
Germany, Leipzig 6, 9, 16
Gewandhaus 6, 12, 15
Joachim, Joseph 29
Liszt, Franz 19
Paris 16
Schumann, Robert 12, 20–26, 29
Vienna 19, 20